THE COUPLE'S GUIDE TO PARENTING

THE COUPLE'S GUIDE TO PARENTING

Maintaining Love Amidst Challenges

AVERY NIGHTINGALE

Creative Quill Press

CONTENTS

CHAPTER 1

Introduction

Expecting that a baby will bring us closer together is a hidden and unrealistic expectation of many couples. In fact, child rearing puts a strain on relationship because of changes in roles and routines, finances and physical and emotional fatigue. Research has shown a decline in relationship satisfaction from the birth of the first child through the raising of teens. High levels of marital satisfaction are shown to return when the children leave home. These findings are not meant to discourage us from parenthood, but rather to show that the transition to parenthood brings both joys and challenges to our family and our relationship. By acknowledging this we can avoid the trap of believing that the difficulties we face are unique and that problems are a result of personal failure. Understanding that there are common patterns to the challenges couples face can help us to strengthen and maintain our relationship through difficult times.

In the beginning, it is important to sort out our feelings about having children. Many of us question ourselves about the right time to have a baby. Even those who feel ready still face fears about how a baby will change our lives. Will we lose our freedom? Will we ever have sex again? Parents are rarely in complete agreement about having a baby, which is quite normal given that each of us has a unique combination of desires and fears about parenthood. Both partners should have a chance to talk about their concerns and be honest about their feelings. Taking the time to sort out these concerns and expectations will help us to support each other through the transition to parenthood.

CHAPTER 2

Understanding the Challenges of Parenting

To varying degrees, everyone's freedom and autonomy decrease with the arrival of children. Children are inescapably needy, and a parent must rearrange their work schedule and personal priorities to accommodate the demands of their children. The freedom to go where you please and do what you want is limited by money and child care options. So, the couple who is used to traveling extensively, trying new adventures, and enjoying common interests together could become disillusioned with family life if they do not maintain a strong partner focus and find ways to continue similar activities with children in tow. Many parents give up an identity they had apart from their children and each other. While reducing involvement in other roles is sometimes necessary for dealing with job and increased family responsibilities, complete identity loss leads to feelings of resentment and depression. This is not beneficial to parents or their children, and it is unnecessary.

Since challenges are an integral part of parenthood, it is important to know what lies ahead for you and your partner so that you can be prepared. It is important not to view the discussions on the next several pages as a list of "bad things that will happen to you if you have kids". Everyone's experience with changes and challenges in family life is different. Some people sail through the transition to parenthood with nary a regret, while others find themselves overmatched by the demands of children. Each challenge that we present here is a way for you and your partner to realistically look at your expectations of becoming parents and compare them to others' experiences. Understanding and preparing for these changes will allow you and your partner to maintain closeness, in your affection for each other and in your orientation as a family.

CHAPTER 3

Communication Strategies for Couples

Maintaining a good marriage means creating time to talk in meaningful ways. Set aside time on a regular basis when enthusiasm levels are still quite high. For some couples, this can be after dinner, for others a glass of wine together after the kids are in bed, and some might prefer to do it first thing in the morning. No matter the time, the first rule is to make it stress-free. If communication time consistently ends in arguments, it will soon be stopped altogether. Pick a topic that is not often lightweight or contentious, and take turns being the speaker and the listener. Avoid making comments or reading into what is being said until it's time to switch roles. Aim to understand each other's thoughts and feelings, even if they differ from your own. This kind of communication can be an incredibly fruitful exercise but isn't predictable. At times, the listener will need to stop seeking resolution to the topic and simply offer empathy to the other's feelings. This is also fine. The first step in solving problems is to understand each other's perspective. Once the problem has been fully understood by both parties, it can be solved and then put away.

Without a doubt, the most crucial factor in your survival as a husband and wife, and also the most challenging, is to sustain a high quality of communication. For many couples, verbal exchange becomes constrained to logistical details and discussions about the children with the uncommon emotional communication that is generally a joke or a war. Regularly, we are so tired at the end of the day that having a meaningful conversation looks as if too much work. Strained of mental and emotional strength, we're often content to sit barely touching each other while we zone out to some mindless TV show. But at the core of the committed relationship is the connection between two people, and that connection is based on ongoing communication. Essential decisions about parenting and handling the kids also can't take place without a healthy dose of talking things through. If a couple loses the ability to communicate well, they will quickly lose their ability to parent effectively.

CHAPTER 4

Balancing Parenting and Relationship

The whole idea of giving to the relationship is based on the strength that comes from maintaining the integrity of the family unit. Above all, a healthy relationship between parents is vital for good parenting. Children are extremely sensitive to tensions and emotions and will be deeply affected by any serious disharmony between you and your partner. At the same time, children can be a source of stress in a relationship and the quality of parenting may suffer when the parents are not getting on well. Finding a balance between the needs of the children and the needs of your relationship with your partner is a complex task. It has its ups and downs and it will almost certainly take a lot of time and effort, but it is an investment which is bound to reap rewards.

I'm sure you're all aware of the vicious cycles many new parents can find themselves in. "I'm too tired for anything" and "Why can't you help me out once in a while?" or perhaps "We never talk about anything anymore, we're just parents."

CHAPTER 5

Nurturing Love and Intimacy

A fulfilling sex life has its health benefits and is the ultimate form of intimacy as it is exclusive to your partner. Plan things around the kids to ensure energy you may have lost during the day is regained – it can be worth the while. Keep in mind that dating and romancing shouldn't stop just because you're married. Kick it up a notch – romance each other. This is a way to show your partner that you still have what it takes to win his/her love and affection. And last but not least, none of us like to be taken for granted. It's simple – say "I love you".

Intimacy is the key for any successful relationship and can be maintained in many simple ways. Romantic touches, hand holding, hugging, kissing – all provide simple but effective ways to show one another that you are still physically attracted to your partner. Plan time alone with one another – and then plan it some more. This strategy can act as your motivation to get through hectic weeks. Be it a date at a restaurant, weekend getaway or an hour at home after the kids are in bed, having intimate alone time keeps the fires burning and emotional bond strong.

With all the pressures of parenting, it's easy for couples to ignore love and intimacy. There may be times when you feel too tired for romance, but a loving relationship can be the one constant in your lives that makes everything else easier and more enjoyable. Making your relationship a priority will help you provide a loving, secure, and happy home for your family.

CHAPTER 6

Managing Conflict and Disagreements

The first type of conflicts are when arguments get out of hand and bad feelings are left. If couples are fighting about something small, the disagreements will often turn nasty. The first step towards preventing this is for the involved party to stop the argument, calm down, and then revisit the topic at a later stage. Another method is to take a time out or break when things are getting heated, with an agreement to revisit the topic once both parties have calmed down. This needs to be done in a positive manner and not seen as an avoidance pattern.

So, how are conflicts managed? What can be done to aid disagreements and prevent marriage breakdown? First, we must identify the difference in which couples' conflicts are about. The type of conflict will determine the management strategies.

Managing conflict and disagreements: When two people come together, conflicts or misunderstandings are bound to happen. There is simply no way around it. The crucial issue is the way in which couples manage these conflicts. Whether the arguments will end with increased understanding towards each other or with a drive further apart will all depend on how conflicts are managed. The latter can be detrimental for couple relationships and damaging for family life.

CHAPTER 7

Supporting Each Other's Parenting Styles

Listen to each other's concerns about your children. Regular communication about the children can often fall by the wayside amidst the infinite tasks and chores that come with parenting. Try to have regular discussions about what is working and what isn't. If possible, set some time aside each week to sit down and discuss your children. They will benefit from having parents who are on the same page and a weekly meeting provides a neutral forum for expression and problem solving. Be open to constructive criticism and try not to be defensive. You are both working hard and want what is best for your children. Listening to your partner's advice may provide insight that you hadn't seen before. At the same time, it's important to pick your battles. You are unlikely to agree on every single aspect of parenting and trying to force your partner into your own style can cause animosity. It is better to agree to disagree on some points.

Even if you discuss and agree on the philosophical aspects of your parenting styles ahead of time, it's not cut and dry. One parent may have difficulty seeing the other implement a non-spanking policy when their own childhood was 'spare the rod, spoil the child'. There is no blueprint that will enable you to perfectly mesh your parenting styles. It is a continuous work in progress. The key is to be supportive and respectful of each other. If you openly degrade the other's parenting style, there is a good chance that you will cause a division in your relationship that can lead to parenting separately and, in the worst case scenario, divorce.

CHAPTER 8

Finding Quality Time as a Couple

Plan a regular weekly or bi-weekly date. Take turns to plan what you will do and keep it a secret if you can. If the kids are old enough, let them know you are going on a date and when they are in bed, the babysitter arrives. This is great for the children to see that maintaining a relationship is important and it means for the two of you, the transition from parenting time to alone time is much easier on your children if you are leaving the house. A weekly golf game for Dad or a scrapbooking club for Mum really isn't the same as spending time together, away from home.

The following are suggestions for finding time to spend alone with your partner.

Perhaps you can't imagine another night out with your partner, but without the children. Or a day trip to a local attraction. Maybe you and your partner aren't even convinced you can spend an afternoon alone together in the house. Many parents feel they don't have enough time with the kids, let alone time alone.

Our calendars are usually filled with the children's activities and playdates, doctor's appointments, and community events. Where are we?

CHAPTER 9

Coping with Stress and Exhaustion

Parenting is a tough job in the best of times, and when parents are tired and stressed, they are less able to handle the normal difficulties of life. Taking care of children can be very stressful, especially when parents have their own personal problems or are feeling overwhelmed by life's responsibilities. Stress can affect the whole family, and it is especially hard on relationships between parents. [...] Below are a number of suggestions for dealing with stress which can have a positive effect on your whole family. Going through them all might seem overwhelming in itself! It could be best to start by looking at the most practical changes and [...] decide what you think will be manageable and have the most importance for a happier family life.

• Recognize the symptoms of stress. • Address the source of the stress. • Work in partnership with your spouse and family. • Practice good health habits. • Give and receive support from friends. • Consider professional help.

CHAPTER 10

Prioritizing Self-Care

Find what energizes and fulfills you outside of parenting. These activities can become your anchor. Family commitments, calling, or fatigue might mean it's not always possible to indulge in these passions frequently, but having them in your life and making time for them when the opportunity arises will help retain your individual identity and feel like time outside of parent duties is time well spent. So take up your old hobby or try a new one! Whether it's sport, dancing, painting, or a Sudoku puzzle, there's always something to be done, and gaining momentum with activities like these can create a sense of achievement.

Parenthood is a lifelong journey, and as such, it's important to maintain energy and passion for the long road ahead. We've all heard the expression "You can't pour from an empty cup," and this is exactly the point. Far from being selfish, self-care makes you a better parent. Constantly being on and vigilant can lead to burnout and exhaustion, and no one functions well as a parent when they're feeling either of those. So how can you keep your cup full and maintain mental and physical energy? What creates energy and passion can be different for different people, so this is a personal journey, but here are some ways you can consider working on maintaining momentum in this demanding role while still feeling that the relationship with your partner and within your family is time well spent.

CHAPTER 11

Building a Strong Co-Parenting Partnership

By following these simple steps and regularly referring to our guide, you will be well on your way to developing a strong and beneficial co-parenting partnership. Remember, it's not about your relationship with your ex; it's about your children and your relationship with them.

6. Be flexible: If you don't agree on something, try to accommodate your ex-partner's approach. There may be more than one solution, and coming to a resolution may involve some give and take.

5. Support generously: Aim to be supportive of your child interacting with the other parent, unless there is a risk of serious harm. This is also true with your ex-partner as a parent, and doing so makes co-parenting easier for both of you. Non-cooperation leads to suspicion and a lack of trust, both of which will diminish the effectiveness of co-parenting.

4. Start where you are: Begin with the existing relation or communication level with your ex-partner. It may not be suitable for

private, face-to-face conversations. Consider using it as a stepping-stone to more personal conversation down the track.

3. Be the team: A separated set of parents is like a team of which both sides have a captain. Make decisions together and act as a united force; cooperation from both parents builds trust and consistency for the children. A great way to conceptualize this team is to schedule regular meetings or calls to discuss the child's needs and how you can meet them. Keep the conversations focused on the child and avoid anything that will lead into an argument. If things do get heated, take a break and come back to the conversation later.

2. Make the relationship with your child the priority: This is your main concern; the well-being of the children. They need to know that both parents are still in their lives and that the separation isn't because of them. Allow your child to open up about their feelings surrounding the situation and validate their feelings. They may be feeling torn between loyalty to both parents. Allow them to have and openly express these feelings. Showing understanding and support for the child's feelings will pay off in building a solid relationship with them.

1. Separate feelings from behavior: It is okay to be hurt and angry, but do not express these emotions to the children. Find healthy ways to release the feelings, like engaging in physical activity or private time.

The steps to successful co-parenting: Despite the many challenges, it is possible to develop an amicable working relationship with your ex for the betterment of your children. For the sake of your kids' well-being, successful co-parenting will involve respectful communication, clear agreements, and flexibility. With these in place, a strong working partnership can be developed.

In building the co-parenting partnership, focus on the long-term goal of having both parents involved in the children's lives. This task is not easy, especially if the parents are angry with one another. Try to put feelings aside and focus on the children. Coping with relationship changes after separation or divorce takes time. Each parent and child will go through the adjustment at their own pace. Your patience, reassurance, and listening ear can minimize tension as children learn to cope with new circumstances.

CHAPTER 12

Dealing with External Influences

It is important to stand united on this so as not to cause conflict between yourselves because other influences can cause stress and tension in your relationship. Take a unified stance and agree not to let external influences cause conflict between you. Confidence in your own abilities will take time, but the more you believe in yourselves, the less you will feel the need to explain your decisions to others. Anyone questioning your choices in parenting. To avoid making a bigger issue than it needs to be, it is wise to give a short and simple answer which does not open the topic for discussion. The decision you make together is what you feel is best for your own child and therefore must be respected.

Raising children in our world today requires a great amount of thought, planning, and energy as new parents. It is not uncommon to be swayed by others' opinions on what to do and how to do it, gained from their own experiences. Most often, these pieces of advice, which are relayed with the best intentions, contradict one another and add to the confusion. It is therefore important to develop the skills to sift through the advice that is given and utilize only that which we feel is of benefit to our own situation.

CHAPTER 13

Maintaining Individual Identities

It is important for each partner to maintain his or her individual identity outside of the marriage. Parents who maintain a sense of individualism are less likely to become resentful of the sacrifices parenting requires. Fathers who maintain a strong sense of individualism are also more likely to have children who take an active role in childrearing. Women who can maintain a sense of independence and balance their needs with their children's and husband's are more likely to keep their marriage satisfying and less emotionally taxing. It is important for couples to support and encourage each other in their individual interests and to take some time apart from their parenting responsibilities to foster these interests. A couple who can balance time with family, work, and recreational time for each individual is likely to maintain a strong marital relationship.

CHAPTER 14

Strengthening the Emotional Connection

Based in part on Gottman's research, couples can implement a variety of strategies to maintain their emotional connection during the new parent period. Regular sharing of the details of each other's lives can be achieved by setting a regular time to sit and talk, perhaps over a cup of tea or a glass of wine after the children are in bed. An inexpensive and effective method of maintaining your partner's awareness of your daily life is a journal that you write to each other, passing it back and forth when you see each other. Each can strive to express fondness and admiration by making a habit of sharing positive thoughts about each other that they have had during the day. This might be done over dinner or through leaving sticky notes in lunch bags or on the fridge. Small acts of kindness and consideration can be facilitated by simple gestures such as brewing a cup of coffee for your partner and staying mindful of his or her likes and dislikes when doing small favors. With all of these strategies, couples should recognize that consistency is more important than the quantity of the interaction, given the time constraints and fatigue that often come with parenting.

A third strategy is to carry out small acts of kindness and consideration, both routine and spontaneous, that let your partner know you are thinking of him or her. Each of these strategies contributes to maintaining a strong emotional bond, or sense of friendship, with your partner. This in turn helps you work as an effective team for dealing with parenting stress. Because that strong friendship means knowing and caring for each other, it also makes it less likely that couples will inadvertently hurt each other as they work through the challenges of parenting. For instance, in one study, Gottman and his colleagues found that new parents were able to communicate their concerns about the sharing of parenting responsibilities without creating negativity in the conversation if they had a strong friendship to begin with.

A second step is to express fondness and admiration for each other. This involves a deliberate focus on your partner's positive traits and acts, and a practice of verbalizing appreciation. Gottman relates this to the early days of dating when couples will constantly express their affection for each other.

Marital researcher and therapist John Gottman has identified strategies for maintaining emotional connection, which are particularly relevant to the transition to parenthood. He advises the development of what he calls "love maps", where partners stay connected to each other's worlds, knowing the details of each other's lives, and being constantly curious to learn more. He found that during the stressful new parent period, when couples are at highest risk for relationship deterioration, partners are not being very aware of what stresses their partner is currently facing, and are not being very supportive of those concerns.

Continuing to feel connected with your partner on an emotional level is key to maintaining a fulfilling relationship. It also enables you both to function as a good parenting team, providing the personal and emotional resources your children need. Finally, it is a gift to your children to show them what a loving, supportive relationship looks like.

CHAPTER 15

Overcoming Parenting Differences

Manage your emotions. It is okay to disagree and normal for any couple to hold differing views on a certain issue. It is unrealistic to expect to agree on every issue. However, frequent and intense conflict between parents can have a negative effect on the children. High levels of conflict are associated with children feeling less secure and less confident in their relationship with their parents. They are also prone to developing behavioral problems. So remember, it is not the difference of opinion that has a harmful effect on children, it is the way the conflict is managed. Try to stay focused on the issue and avoid blaming and general criticism. This allows a discussion to be more productive and increases the chance of a resolution.

Build a bridge. In order to bring about change in an area of difficulty, a supportive environment must be created. Research shows that change occurs more successfully when the focus is on the positive things that are already taking place, or that have taken place in the past. It is the ability to identify positive interactions even on an unrelated issue that gives a couple confidence that they can work together as parents. The underlying confidence stems from knowing that they have the skills; it is just a matter of applying them to a different aspect of their parenting.

Understanding parenting styles. For some, talking about parenting differences is synonymous with criticizing each other's way of being a parent. However, discussing different methods of parenting does not necessarily mean that they are judging or criticizing the other's parenting style. Taking a personality approach can help. It is important to recognize that your parenting style might be a reflection of your personality. However, personality noting that someone's personality successfully reflects on their parenting style allowing them to be more effective at parenting, if you are aware of adapting your approach to suit the needs of your child. This makes it easier to appreciate each other's position. The key to successful parenting is being able to adapt your style in order to best meet the needs of your child.

CHAPTER 16

Resolving Financial Challenges

Fast losses of income, debt, or unexpected expenses can be catastrophic if a parent/parents do not have good financial management skills or the ability to manage the family's income, spending, and related financial matters. This can be the final straw for many couples and can be a cause of family breakup. Debt and low income have led to increased levels of stress and parent conflict. Debt is also strongly linked to a higher incidence of child abuse, either through intentional harm, neglect, or the use of harsher parenting techniques. This behavior can hinder a child's progress and development. A study executed in the USA in 1995 shows a strong correlation between child abuse and low income. It is generally accepted that poverty and financial hardship put a family under extra stress, and this increases the likelihood of family dysfunction. A child's development and progress can be hindered in ways that are difficult to correct at a later time. This can cause great disappointment for a parent, for example, being unable to afford good schooling materials with no means of catching up. Risen inflation rates and a decline in the value of welfare are causes of concern for modern-day parents.

Financial challenges are increasing rapidly for soon-to-be and current parents. The burden of saving up for college, medical care, the checkups of a child, and other related necessities is bound to be more stressful if the amount of money being spent by parents is not in good financial standing. The financial security and well-being of a family can be a good indicator of overall family functioning.

CHAPTER 17

Creating a Supportive Network

The cultural or class differences between family members and friends can sometimes be a source of problems in marriage due to conflicting opinions on how to parent a child or the range of acceptable behavior in our children. You and your partner may disagree on what is and isn't acceptable. It is important through these difficult times that you keep communication open and empathize with each other. If you can understand your partner's feelings about a situation and 'why' they feel that way, then it is more likely that you can come to a compromise or a tolerant agreement on your different beliefs. The support of understanding friends can be a big help during these times.

One of the most important steps you can take to absorb the shock of parenting is to build a supportive network for yourself and your marriage. Developing a community of friends, family, and expert advisors can help lighten the load on you and your partner. The experience of pregnancy, birth, and parenting brings with it a flood of emotions. Normally, both positive and negative emotions are experienced, and often they are conflicting. New parents need a lot of support and understanding. No one person can be everything others need, so it is important that you widen your network and give some thought as to what kinds of support you need and who can best provide it.

CHAPTER 18

Sharing Household Responsibilities

Your aim is to do something that most couples actually fail to do - share your lives together and bring up your children without any-one's quality of life being compromised. Sounds great in theory but it's an immense task. The simultaneous tasks of running a house-hold, holding down one or more jobs and being a parent can leave you both feeling overloaded and overtired. For most people, the honeymoon of shared parenthood disappears with the nighttime feeds and nappy changes. You wake up one morning and realize that for over a month you have not had a conversation with your partner that has not revolved around household duties or children. At this critical juncture, it is time to sit down and talk about how you are going to be parents and breadwinners and ensure that you are both fulfilled in these challenging roles. You may have to choose the time when neither of you is excessively busy with work; you may even have to sacrifice a night's television. This "big leap" requires increased awareness of what the other is doing and what needs to be done. It may also involve a reduction in work hours and joint planning to pursue a less lucrative but more family-friendly lifestyle.

1. Goals 2. Assumptions 3. The Big Leap 4. What's the difference? 5. Time management 6. Household Delegation 7. Housework - what needs doing and what it's worth 8. Avoiding Anger as a Tool 9. House meeting/fair 10. The Fair Fighting Act 11. What to do with free time 12. Payment 13. If all else fails 14. Additional information for step-families. 15. Summary

CHAPTER 19

Parenting Through Different Life Stages

1. INFANCY: It's the first stage of a child's life, which is from birth to the age of 2 years. An infant is completely unaware of what is happening in his environment. This is the time when parents have to make extra effort to understand their child. Confidence between parent and child is very important for the upbringing of a child. The behavior of a child at this stage depends upon his birth order and number of siblings. If a child is the only child of his parents, it is usually found that he is more aggressive as compared to the child who has siblings. If parents have access to good information, they can compare their child's behavior with others. This is the only stage in which parents and their children can spend most of the time with each other. In other stages, their children will get busy in their life and don't have much time for their parents. So this is the best time to build a strong parent-child relationship. At this stage, children need to be parent-centered, have a reliable routine, a secure and clean environment, and recognition of

a child's communication. Because of the beautiful and innocent nature of a child at this stage, parents always want to keep their child as their children, but time always flies and no one can stop it.

In our society, students and children are familiar with these words because they are also passing through various stages of life. Parents can bring up their children in a better way if there is proper planning of their life. Planning is essential to meet the needs and requirements of your child at different life stages. Parents these days are well aware of their child's life stages because of the standard of education. Basically, there are 5 stages of life. These are: Infancy, Early Childhood, Middle Childhood, Adolescence, and Young Adulthood. The period of each stage may vary, but recent research says that children who are living in the western world, especially in the UK, are spending 2-3 years at each stage of life.

CHAPTER 20

Recognizing and Addressing Burnout

According to a recent study, post-natal depression in fathers and mothers occurs in 52% and 39%. These statistics, while quite alarming, clearly indicate the problems which arise out of the stress and emotional burnout that comes from managing a family. All too often, we are absorbed by our children and work and postpone marital relations. This creates an imbalance which increases the possibility of either parent feeling overwhelmed with duties. As parents, you have a bigger workload, less time for yourselves and recreational activities, decreased privacy, and romance. All of these are factors that contribute towards emotional burnout and can affect your relationship. Left unchecked, stress and burnout lead to anger, rages, depression, and substance abuse. Most parents are unaware of the dramatic effect their stressful behavior has on children. Discuss the signs of burnout and stress between yourselves and create an action plan to remedy the situation – find ways to share responsibilities so both of you have free time. It is well understood that happy parents create a happy family. Periodically check for burnout symptoms, be aware of the effect it is having on your relationship and your children, and take steps to control and prevent further damage. Work towards creating a low-stress environment for your family – it will be beneficial to both yourselves and your children in the long run.

CHAPTER 21

Fostering a Positive Parenting Environment

• Identify your goals and what you want to do. Parents need to sit down and really think about what they want to achieve long term, and then from this, identify their goals as a parent. Setting goals helps you stay focused and provides insight into what you need to achieve your goal. An example of a goal: One goal a parent might set would be to create a warm and happy home environment that is child-centered and provides good role modeling. Volunteer a couple of hours each month to support a child-based activity outside the home. This will give an opportunity to practice what you are advocating and provide a new dimension to your family life. These activities can then be gauged against the environment you are trying to create. • Understand a child's behavior is linked to your reaction. For every action, there is a reaction. All behavior is a form of communication. We need to know what the child is communicating and then give them the appropriate answer. Often the meaning of the message is below the behavior. An example of this could be a child may be disturbing a parent from getting some work done. At face value, the message is unhelpful; however, the child may be feeling left out and is striving for attention. • Be consistent and fair. Children need to know what's going to happen the next time they engage in a certain behavior. If your reaction is sometimes negative, but sometimes not, the child is likely to take the risk and see if they can get the positive result. • Avoid smothering your child with overprotection and over-indulgence. The child who receives a new toy every time they go shopping with a parent is being set up for problems later in life. Giving to a child without receiving effort/behavior from the child is like having a blank check. Children do best when they have to work for what they receive. An example could be using a reward system. When the child has a positive goal-directed behavior or a successful school report, they can then receive a reward. Or in another situation, it may be to ignore a certain behavior and then praise the child when they change it. For example, a child is able to tie shoelaces when shown but does not yet have the skill mastered. The parent may ignore the child's attempts to get them to tie the laces and praise in a few days' time when the child has a better chance of success.

CHAPTER 22

Enhancing Problem-Solving Skills

Similar to good listening skills, successful problem-solving is built on a foundation of effective communication. Problems cannot be solved if they are not known, and effective communication helps the problem to be clearly understood. It is also difficult to solve a problem if only one person's view of it is explored. Problems that couples bring to their relationship are generally co-owned, and solutions are likely to be more effective if both are involved in their formulation. So, having effective communication means having an effective way of exploring problems from both people's perspectives.

Each couple faces numerous problems in their daily life. Successful problem-solving skills are obviously the key to creating a fulfilling life. This is also a very important aspect of the couple's relationship. How they solve problems not only influences the nature of their life together but also how they feel about each other. There are clear relationships between the way couples solve problems and the quality of their relationship. For instance, it is now generally accepted that couples who hold their couple relationship in mind during a disagreement are better at sustaining their relationship. Further, couple problem-solving is an area where there is great potential for improvement. We will discuss some ways in which couples may enhance their problem-solving skills.

CHAPTER 23

Embracing Flexibility and Adaptability

Flexibility is closely related to adaptability. Being adaptable in parenting means being able to make changes in response to a child's temperament, age, or developmental stage. It is an ongoing process whereby parents are willing to change the expectations they have for their children, as well as the demands they place upon them. Parents with good adaptability are also open to change in their own behavior as an alternative to trying unsuccessfully to change the child. This does not mean that parents abandon their principles or let the children take over. It is more about recognizing what can and can't be changed and responding effectively to issues that are presented.

Flexibility is the ability to respond to changing circumstances and unpredictability without getting thrown off balance. Parenting is a continuously changing process. Consistency is important for children, but parents must have the flexibility to change the methods of discipline and communication to suit each individual child. Parents who can adjust their expectations in small and large ways will be able to respond more effectively to their children when they do misbehave. Being flexible also means being able to take a break from parenting at the appropriate times and considering the needs of self and partner. Sometimes the best way to solve a problem is to be completely uninvolved in it.

CHAPTER 24

Promoting Open and Honest Communication

Communicating concerns, feelings, and thoughts can be difficult if it has not been happening regularly. In this case, know that it is okay to take these things slow. Choose an active time to talk while doing some sort of activity and have a relaxed attitude so that no one feels pressured. When discussing problems or concerns, it may be helpful to focus on just one problem at a time. This will avoid both partners becoming overwhelmed, and the aim to solve one problem before moving on to another will be more attainable. It is also essential that the goal of this conversation is to improve the relationship. This may seem like a no-brainer; however, much communication can become negative with one partner attacking the other or the problem at hand. Do not lose sight of the understanding that both partners want what's best for their relationship and family.

1. Schedule regular alone time to talk. 2. Avoid interrupting and listen for understanding. 3. Be honest and sensitive to others' feelings. This means taking time to think about what we really

mean to say and how the other might receive it. 4. Avoid criticizing and act as a team. 5. Use "I" statements to express thoughts, feelings, and ideas. 6. When you express a problem, also express possible solutions. 7. Solve problems together. 8. Agree to disagree. Recognize that sometimes things cannot be resolved right away. 9. Only give feedback when the other is ready to hear it. 10. Encourage each other to express their feelings and thoughts through praise. ("I'm glad that you can talk to me about this.")

In order to promote and encourage open communication, it is essential that each partner feels like they can openly express their thoughts, feelings, and ideas without fear of rejection or retaliation. Here are some steps to improving communication:

CHAPTER 25

Celebrating Milestones and Achievements

Celebrating success at overcoming challenges is an integral part of maintaining a healthy relationship. Many couples get so caught up in the day-to-day hustle of parenting that they forget to recognize their own achievements. However, taking small steps to correct destructive patterns and making changes is a significant accomplishment. It's important to take time to reflect on what was learned through difficult experiences and how the two of you have grown as individuals and as a couple. By acknowledging that you have faced adversity and have become stronger, you can affirm the value of your efforts. Consider celebrating with the kids; this will show them that it's possible to learn from mistakes and that effort is deserving of praise. For example, planning a family outing after a particularly rough patch at home can symbolize a fresh start and the mending of hard feelings. An important example to set for your children is that family members are in a constant state of learning and that it's okay to make mistakes as long as we take responsibility for them. By using difficult experiences as a chance for growth and assessing what changes can be made, families can emerge stronger and wiser.

CHAPTER 26

Seeking Professional Help and Guidance

The decision to seek professional help is another major milestone. In order to facilitate their child's growth and well-being, a couple must take care to protect their own mental health. This may require counseling, therapy, or ongoing support from friends and family. There are countless resources available to parents. Do the research and don't sell yourself short. If you feel you could benefit from professional help, then you probably can. This should not be overlooked or taken lightly. Therapy and counseling can be expensive, but many find it is well worth it as they regain the ability to live life to the fullest and enjoy their family. A mental health professional can also be very helpful in assessing "where do we go from here?" They can help define parenting goals and provide direction for attaining them. For parents of a child with a disability, there are services available to help them find someone to care for their child while they engage in a few hours of respite care. This break is essential for maintaining emotional health.

CHAPTER 27

Strengthening the Parent-Child Relationship

As one man puts it, "The problem with this generation is not that they disobey their parents, it's that they don't consider it necessary to obey us." The tragic part is that many parents do not even realize the breakdown in the relationship with their children. They are lulled into complacency until a crisis or frightening situation with their child jerks them into the reality of their lack of communication and connection with their children.

When we realize our role as parents to our children, we will see the necessity of a strong parent-child relationship. We need to be able to influence our children to follow the right path in their lives. When there is no relationship, there is no real connection—there is no mutual respect. Where there is relationship, there is influence. If a child does not have a strong relationship with his parents, he may look for influence in other places—even from a stranger.

CHAPTER 28

Establishing Boundaries and Routines

It is essential to agree upon a set of discipline guidelines (house rules). Without these, there will be no consistency in child discipline. Behavior that is unacceptable to an adult will often be acceptable in certain situations. This is simply because the child does not understand the implications of his actions. For example, a child could start misbehaving in a public place. His parents, glancing at the disapproving looks from onlookers, will usually let the behavior continue because they are unwilling to stop and make a scene. Unbeknownst to the child, he has just been given the green light to misbehave in public.

Randomness is the enemy of family teamwork. Remember how effective your teamwork as a couple was? If children have the power to create randomness, then they will if given half a chance. Couple teamwork cannot be sustained without well-established routines and secure boundaries for children. Parents' intentions are good, but sometimes a child can persuade you to change a boundary. Be clear about boundaries and be consistent. This is much easier said than done, but inconsistency over a few boundary changes will result in chaos.

CHAPTER 29

Balancing Work and Family Life

For those families who find it difficult to balance the demands of work and family, the first step is to take a careful look at how time is being spent. Often with both parents working, or a single parent holding down two jobs, there is a feeling of never having enough time or energy left over for the children. One or both parents might feel guilty and overcompensate by allowing the child too much free rein or material possessions. Unfortunately, the overcompensating parent(s) is often too tired and harried to monitor the child's activities or set limits—thus the child gets his or her needs met, but at the expense of being left alone too much with too few guidelines. This can indicate a chronic lack of family time and the child's needs for parental guidance and disciplinary action.

Maintaining emotional warmth in the family while dealing with the stresses of work and parenting is not easy. The two major time-consuming areas of employment (occupational or professional work and childrearing) can present considerable challenges to parents in the realm of family life. Many families successfully juggle the demands of career and child care while preserving time together as a couple and a family. Others find the task of dividing time and energy between work and family to be daunting and overwhelming.

CHAPTER 30

Emphasizing the Importance of Teamwork

Look for ways to share small moments together throughout the day to help you feel connected. Have a cup of tea together after the kids are in bed, or take 5 minutes to sit and chat while the baby plays. Touching base in little ways can help you to still feel like a couple, rather than two people who just share the responsibilities of parenting. Often it's the little things that keep us feeling connected. Scheduling a regular date night is also a great way to stay close, and it's especially important if you have let your relationship slip as a low priority. Hire a sitter or trade childcare with a friend and use the time to enjoy each other's company. It can be difficult at first to justify spending time and money on a date when you have young children, but it's a lot cheaper than marriage counseling in the long run!

Parenting is a tough job and it can take a toll on your relationship with your partner if you let it. Here's what you can do to make sure it brings you closer together instead of driving you apart. First, realize that you and your partner are a team; you're in this together. Keep that thought firmly in your mind when things get tough. Approach difficulties as something you can solve together to do what's best for your child, rather than looking at each other as the cause of the problem. Keeping the idea of teamwork in the forefront will help you to support one another in the roles you take on and foster a sense of unity in tackling parenting issues, which is crucial to staying close and not letting resentment drive a wedge between you.

CHAPTER 31

Sustaining Love and Connection in the Long Run

The remaining sections of this book will focus on specific issues and parenting stages, but it is important not to lose sight of the "big picture." Over the years, the two of you have committed to having a family together; parents' devotion to their children is honorable and important. However, your primary identity is still as a couple. Research consistently shows that the quality of the couple's relationship has a powerful effect on parenting and on children's development. Children feel secure when they know their parents are united and when they are convinced of their parents' love for each other. Remember, the family exists to support the growth and development of each member, but the strength of the family is based on the strength of the couple. We have gone through some specific examples of challenges encountered by parenting couples. Through using the ideas and tools we have provided in this book, you can approach one another with understanding and compassion, to help overcome some of these challenges in ways that strengthen your connection. This is not only beneficial for the two of you, but also serves as a positive model for your children. But there are countless issues you will face that have not been mentioned. Think of the examples described here as a template for problem solving. When new issues arise, make an effort to understand each other's experience and perspective, and work together to find a resolution that feels right to both of you. The most important thing is to keep the lines of communication open. As long as you are connecting with one another, you will continue to learn and grow as a couple. And remember, it is not the specific method or solution that is most important; staying connected through the process is what maintains the bond between you. This is the love that your children will see and feel, and the best gift you can give to them.

CHAPTER 32

Conclusion

In subsequent visits with Bob and Lisa, it became clear that their marriage and sanity were being tested by a variety of factors related to their parenting and work responsibilities. Lisa expressed frustration at the difficulty of finding time to do a proper job of caring for Jenny and of balancing the care of the home and the child. Oftentimes, Bob and Lisa had perceived each other's behavior toward Jenny as misdirected or as being indicative of differing long-term goals concerning child-rearing. On occasion, Jenny's behavior and the problems posed by the effort to discipline an infant would lead to tension, a sense of helplessness, and even feelings of guilt on the part of Lisa and Bob. The situation was a far cry from the tranquil, gratifying picture of child-rearing Bob and Lisa had once envisioned. At times, they wondered if it was possible to change things for the better and to find a sense of fulfillment and unity in their shared commitment to Jenny.

It was a bright, warm day in May that found Laurel and me at Robert and Lisa's home in Lexington, Kentucky. Jenny was an adorable six-month-old, and, although we didn't know it at the time, Jenny would make her mark on the course of this book. Bob and

Lisa, modern-day yuppies, were a dual-income couple with a beautiful new home they were eager to show us. We sat in the living room while Jenny scooted around our feet. Lisa told Laurel and me that Jenny was spending three days a week at a nearby daycare center. It was evident, however, that Lisa was not entirely comfortable with the arrangement. A few minutes later, Bob privately told me that he felt Lisa was being overly rough on Jenny in her attempts to make Jenny assert her will.